Of Whiskey & Winter

Of Whiskey
& Winter

Peter Conners

WHITE PINE PRESS / BUFFALO, NEW YORK

Copyright ©2007 by Peter Conners

All rights reserved. This work, or portions thereof, may not be reproduced in any form without the written permission of the publisher.

Grateful appreciation to the journals and publications where the following poems first appeared or are forthcoming, occasionally in different form:

100 Contemporary Prose Poems (China): "American Prose Poet"; *An Introduction to the Prose Poem:* "American Prose Poet"; *City Newspaper:* "The Poet Washes Dishes," "Valentine," "A Girl"; *Drunken Boat:* "The Great Undertoad of Cape Cod," "Beach Head"; *Flights:* "Dog Days," "Puberty (Our Arms & Legs Emerge); *In Posse Review:* "Rejoice," "A Letter to My Love;" *Magazine Minima:* "Waiting on a Friend," "Puberty," "Formula for Frustration"; *Mid-American Review:* "Instructions for a Rainy Day," "Kingdom of Worms," "Garbage of the Glittering Sun"; *Mississippi Review:* "Feast of the Wounded Bird"; *Mosaico* (Amman, Jordan): "Gathering" in English/Arabic translation; *Poetry International:* "Rejoice"; *The Potomac:* "The Wonderment We Bypassed"; *Salt Hill:* "Endurance," "The Dog Goes Bow-wow," "The Thing Behind the Other Thing," "Kingdom of the Silver Hairbrush"; *Sentence:* "Gathering," "American Prose Poet," "Huey," "Peter Means Rock"; *Sudden Stories: A Mammoth Anthology of Minuscule Fiction:* "A Girl"; *Two Rivers Review:* "Checking on Whitman"; *Unpleasant Event Schedule:* "Chromo Boy," "But Not Today," "My Cat Recites a Poem."

An earlier version of the section, The Names of Winter, was published as a chapbook by FootHills Publishing in Winter 2004.

"Beyond The Dream," "Valentine, Dropping," and "A Girl" were featured on the radio program *Fiction in Shorts* on public radio, WXXI 91.5 FM Rochester, NY.

"The Babies of Winter" and "The Poet Washes Dishes" were featured on the radio program *What's The Word?* on public radio, WXXI 91.5 FM Rochester, NY.

Publication of this book was made possible, in part, by a grant from the National Endowment for the Arts, which believes that a great nation deserves great art, and with public funds from the New York State Council on the Arts, a State Agency.

First Edition.

Printed and bound in the United States of America.

13-digit ISBN: 978-1-893996-89-2

Library of Congress Control Number: 2007930473

White Pine Press
P.O. Box 236
Buffalo, New York 14201
www.whitepine.org

◆ ◆ ◆

Thank you to Nin Andrews, Sean Thomas Dougherty, Russell Edson, Peter Johnson, Christopher Kennedy, Naomi Shihab Nye, Daryl Scroggins, and Gary Young for their close readings, encouragement, and invaluable suggestions on this collection. Thank you to Zach Hraber and Cactus May for my web site. Thank you to Steve Smock for creating the painting on the cover of this book and for designing the cover. Thank you to Dennis Maloney & Elaine LaMattina for their care in publishing this book. Love to my family, blood and extended.

—*for Karen*

Contents

TEMPLE OF JUNE BUGS

IN THE BARN

They think they can say everything, blanket the world with assorted words: but all they are saying is "trees." They can't even hold on to the birds who fly off again, and here they are rejoicing in having produced such strange flowers!

—Francis Ponge,
The Cycle Of The Seasons
translated by Beth Archer Brombert

FOREWORD

♦ ♦ ♦

PETER CONNERS' PROSE POETRY is difficult to characterize. This is a good thing, especially at a time when the prose poem-as-genre has become fashionable, almost faddish, and when many prose poems seem predictable, imitations of imitations. Even in 1993 my first assistant editor of *The Prose Poem: An International Journal* quit, saying all the poems sounded the same. I could see her point, but back then we hadn't read the work of Peter Conners. His first prose poetry collection, *Of Whiskey and Winter,* joins the list of a few first books of prose poems (most notably by Mary Koncel, David Shumate, and Lesle Lewis) that read like a selected or greatest hits volume.

Conners himself has written admirably on the prose poem, and his journal, *Double Room,* has become one of the major conduits for reflections on what has come to be known as PP/FF (prose poem/flash fiction). We could argue endlessly whether the poems in *Of Whiskey and Winter* are prose poems or flash fictions or anti-stories or whatever, but this approach would be dumb, mostly because it would overlook the originality of the book. In *Of Whiskey and Winter,* Conners, like many prose poets, pays tribute to and subverts many of the genres the prose poem readily embraces, such as the fable, the letter, the instruction manual, the formula, and the local legend, but the way he accomplishes this difficult task is totally unique. His poems are simultaneously entertaining and disturbing but most of all wonderfully unpredictable, so that throughout this collection, he ends up breathing life into a genre which many critics believe is exhausting itself.

"Certified Alive" is a representative poem from this collection.

CERTIFIED ALIVE

Four pound boots and two pound wool sweaters;
everything is heavy in winter. The physician's
assistant deducts three pounds off the scale for
my quilted cargo pants & thick purple socks:
sweet, grandmotherly, even with a needle. Each
spring I emerge thicker with bear weight. My
hair grows, my waist, my growl a truer lament.
Too many winters, too much weight. This is my
physical, I should be allowed to weep openly. It
is a dirty business, this winter, seeping shitty
grainy slush by the back door. Thermal inserts
overtake sneakers - turn them into quaint coast-
ers for the work of burial, exhumation. This is
the place where I pee in a cup: the waste of
whiskey and winter. It is taken, tested, deemed
healthy piss for the moment. I ask if they will
carry it outside, proclaim my status in a yellow
gush, *Certified Alive*, across the pristine white snow.
They will not, nor with my blood. It will take
till spring to spell the names of my discontent.
And then melt. Half pound hats, quarter pound
gloves; it is a testament that we climb out from

under winter at all. Outside, the walk is buried
beneath a fresh ten inches of snow. The storms
closed in again last night, now later today, at
some point, I must assemble my full winter
weight to shovel a way for the postman to deliver
the last of my test results. If I am too late, only
his shadow will appear.

This is one of those poems where a simple activity is described,
having a yearly physical, yet we know much more is at stake. The
poem begins with a literal heaviness: the heaviness of winter
clothes, the bulkiness of a few winter pounds around the waist,
the oppressiveness of winter itself. But this physical weight
becomes metaphorical and internalized when Conners laments,
"Too many winters, too much weight," and then catalogues some
of winter's indignities, calling this season "a dirty business." Why
"a dirty business"? Why does Conners want to "be allowed to
weep openly" at his physical? Mostly because both situations
remind him of his mortality, of "burial" and "exhumation," of
the fact that his urine test could be a prelude to certifying him
dead instead of alive.

But Conners' genius appears in the way he avoids gloominess
by deftly leaping back and forth between images of winter and
those of his physical. As it turns out, all seems to end well as his
"piss" is eventually "deemed healthy." Granted, the winter contin-
ues to close in and the "walk is buried beneath a fresh ten inches
of snow," but Conners can still "proclaim [his] status" as being
"Certified Alive," while congratulating us all for our ability to
"climb out from under winter." But there is a further irony to the
poem which suggests Conners has already reached a mature style
and vision. He realizes that his urine has passed the test only "for

the moment," and that he must shovel yet more of the "weight" of winter so that the postman can deliver his remaining test results. Will they be as positive as his urine test? There are of course no assurances—instead the unpredictability of life and the necessity to accept that unpredictability. In a sense, then, "certified alive" is a kind of oxymoron because "certified" suggests certainty, an "ensurance," if I may coin a word, that life can't provide.

Conners' celebration of these kinds of complexities and paradoxes occurs throughout *Of Whiskey and Winter.* Sometimes he accepts them, as in "Certified Alive"; other times, he's angry, as in "Twenty-Six Days of Sun" when he complains, "five months without sun is too much to take," or as in "Kingdom of Worms" when he tells us that "Everything comes before death" so it's time to "wear [our] boots and kick the shit out of a dying kingdom today." Perhaps he best describes the give-and-take we call life in "Rejoice," the final poem of this collection.

REJOICE

Postcards, gas bills, love letters tinged with
pheromones. I don't know whether it is an act of
trust or a test of loyalty but people keep giving
me things to mail. This is too much though.
Marked undeliverable. Instead I will sit here
dreaming of packages that open into a future
they will never reveal. Only ritual, only more rit-
ual: cats and dogs poised to hear bell chimes
through a shifting maze of seasons. This nip in
the air. Temple of June Bugs, Kingdom of

Worms; the time of our awaited birth is awash
in new currents, baptized in rivers of whiskey
and winter. Strange flowers planted to pick or
plow under. As you will.

Thus Conners ends on an ambiguous note, leaving us with
images of birth, death, and regeneration clinging to each other, or
perhaps strolling hand-in-hand across his landscape of whiskey
and winter, a landscape we hope he revisits.

—Peter Johnson

THE NAMES OF WINTER

◆ ◆ ◆

The Babies of Winter

It is not just the chill, but the sounds. Information spent on thin
wires of air. Upstairs, the window has been blown open; a dilem-
ma telegraph beating itself against walls that will need to be
painted before the baby arrives. Not a figurative baby, a literal
one: minuscule mittens and woolen hats with chin straps. The
cobwebs will need to be dusted from Whitman's old toys. The
seasons hold us tight: the storms have betrayed our trust but they
must be forgiven. Dusted, put to use. They did the best they
could. They are one hundred years old, and the babies of winter
must always be forgiven.

Untitled

You will open the door to this mystery with the word breath. We will select the word mystery instead of the word eternity because they are all mysterious and always we must breathe this warm and mysterious. The warm and sober breath, the solemn and knowing breath; the lasting breath of satisfaction we have earned in earning our last, so the trickle of moisture that provides mountains with valleys and those with streambeds. I have been told to help you breathe and who am I to point out your previous mastery? There is so little that I can do while we wait to begin this life.

The Rebellion of Fingers

My fingers protest this plot we have shoveled out for ourselves.
They will do as they are ordered but they will do it slowly,
lugubriously, as plows drive fingers through narrow side streets.
They curl and glower at me from their home row perch. It is
laughable, really, this rebellion! I will place them where I wish
regardless of weather; they will need to wither like rotten breath
at my sides before I give up! And so it has come to this: the
gloves, as foretold, have come off. I drag my hands to the banks
and push my naked fingers into dirty ridges the plows have left
behind, these snowy fingerprints of our city. Let fingers touch
fingers, let them lament this rough streak of humanity.

    I am going inside with or without you.

ENDURANCE

Indeed. These jagged crevasses of the psyche are treacherous, gray. Extending two hundred plus days in every direction; an ominous glacier of gloom, this city of whiskey and winter. I am no Shackleton, nor even Orde-Lees of the Imperial Trans-Antarctic Expedition. Who even knew that a predatory seal existed? Curled beneath my comforter, wife asleep beside me, son in blankets and bears, these men place Job in some sandy bliss; fruit drink in one hand, yawning, left foot in honey, right foot in butter. The puppies were skinned and eaten—taste compared to sea leopard, penguin meat! My gusty February wind leaks through poorly insulated cracks, the heating bill higher than need be. This concerns me. And the next day too. No I am no Shackleton, nor even Frank Worsley navigating the tempestuous Drake Passage with broken compass and sextant. In truth, I don't know what a sextant is and would most likely lose it in the kitchen clutter drawer anyway. Manual long since tossed out. No I am no Shackleton, nor even the lowest of those left on Elephant Island to wait. This winter irritates me more than the abscess on Hudson's behind. Leaves me rigid like Blackboro's dead toes dropping one by one into the tin can beneath Dr. McIlroy's careful snips. I admit it, on days when the slate sky threatens to push my spirit through frozen earth, I think of those men and smile. Close the book on them. Leave them on some battered ice floe in the South Atlantic to push the limits of human endurance alone.

SOME FORTRESS OF SOLITUDE

It grew from a solitary crystal. In the scene, our hero marches through tundra in a flimsy parka and schoolboy backpack (no doubt filled with apples, cheese sandwiches, organic sundry dug from Aunt Martha's garden), leaping ice floes, negotiating arctic staircases, until he comes upon the property: glowing, ebullient, a wasteland. He retrieves the predestined sliver from the tangle of fresh carrots and launches it into space...

A polar bear yawns.

A walrus nose sniffs through waves.

Blubber melts to oil.

Our hopes fly with the shard: truth, justice, a room to call one's own. Until the fate of mankind jams a shiv into the belly of eternal winter, erupts into unbreakable minaret fingers soaring miles into the air. Walkways, ballrooms, sculpted ice foyers...

Our hero enters to find his family waiting inside. This last bastion of our Superman contains an unexpected built-in: a perpetual family reunion in every room.

Disheartened, he turns and walks away through the drifts. It is too cold here, the location is horrible—and shouldn't a fortress of solitude be just that?

SNOWBIRDS

My maternal grandparents were snowbirds; the scent of their plumage an evergreen air freshener dangling off the rearview mirror of a Cadillac. As with all snowbirds, they were white. This helped them blend into their creamy plush interior, a southwest trajectory taking them farther into lands of brown and green. The flight of snowbirds flaps to a bossa nova beat: snowbirds, shuffleboard, snowbirds, shuffleboard... There are outposts across America down every alcove into the Baja peninsula; RV nests snug under striped awnings, wafts of hibachi smoke and prime time tv shows an outlet away as gray whales breed and breech a mile offshore. It is amazing what we have learned we need to live with. As a boy perched atop my grandparents' enclosed patio the snowbirds sang out to each other forty feet up through spiny courtyard trees. The call of the snowbirds. Their names have long since turned into historical references—Agnes, Mabel, Cora, Mina—feline frames on swinging link chains, ankles thick with water and weight. Children, grandchildren, signs of the cross: signify the snowbird. My family flew with the snowbirds for years; six of us drafting on eighteen wheeler currents. A paneled station wagon stuffed with swimsuits, snorkels, eye drops and playing cards; despite daily divisions, united in flight. And my grandparents, those snowbirds, greeted us in powder blue plaids, pastels, seldom seen elbows and knees. Lovingly showed us their pool, their games, tidy early bird food and flock. The world of the snowbird. My maternal grandparents were snowbirds, now gone, so forgive me if I see a vision of them through these snowy poem branches: side by side, taking flight, slipping this cold winter cage for the comfort of warmer climes.

All for This

The spiders of December spin frost webs across the windows.
They disappear under direct gaze; illuminated by sly glance alone,
too elusive for a poet or toddler. In the morning, Whitman and I
stare past webs into the avenue, yawn. A yellow piddle mandala.
Three breeds of footprint, one human, no birds at the feeder.
Truck. Yes, truck. *Truck, truck.* Yes, now: *Apple.* Seasons sidle in
while we compile grocery lists; wake up one morning with a
shovel, bed down at night with a spade. This month, my name
split into three. A bottle of warm milk. A fire truck with work-
ing lights. This is what Mondays are for.

The Names of Winter

(Here in this bleak city of Rochester,
Where there are twenty-seven words for "snow,"
Not all of them polite. . . —Anthony Hecht)

Neither one nor the other, we would whisper the name sleet as a child murmurs *mother* to the pale blue glow of sleep through ancestral dowels. In this thick February no sleet or sleep or Yucatan dreams; a thick bed of salt no match for these fat flakes. And so too forlorn loners skirting sidelong past strange atmospheres. Cool, limpid hipster snow makes the scene. Evoke now the orgy of cream. Violet granule hammers. There is no better movie than the timeless drift of eccentric patterned doilies through air; a crisp two a.m. cameo filmed in streetlight aureole, this city of whiskey and winter. If we are to dream ourselves away, let us dream of this....

VALENTINE

She removed the dagger. In the hopes that one day this symbol
would become *true love* she inserted the tip of the blade into the
soft flesh of the birch. She carved their initials together: J.K +
V.L. There is no rejection in the forest. A birch may sustain thou-
sands of cuts without bleeding, but not so a little girl. All the
cuts, all the wounds, all whispered prayers and yearnings are
invisible in the middle of the Forest. The birches there are scarred
with initials dating back to her parents' time. The hearts date
back even longer. It is a forest of stories. Of memory. A place of
temples and sacrifice at once as ancient and fragile and pristine as
love itself. Today—a day for all loves—when she stands perfectly
still with the blade in her hand she can feel the wandering echoes
of history hold their breath along with her. Together they freeze
in anticipation. J.K. + V.L. If it is to begin, it will be today. If it
will be today, it will be forever. At last, the two lines move down-
ward and converge to complete the heart. The arrow comes last,
sharp, unerring, pointed fast at its target. The target flutters and
beats. The target is large and wet and overflowing. The knife
clicks shut, the girl leaves the forest and the branches overhead
sway in a wind so faint it is barely a wind, barely a breeze, but
more the idea of these things together.

Cat Days

If summer has its dog days, then winter is for cats. It is true, I have been too long in this house alone. If spring is for lovers, then winter goes to the recluse. In the name of full disclosure, the two are not mutually exclusive though one must surely precede the other. My cats, two males, snuggle unselfconsciously. Against a backdrop of dead winter they are too serene; more an ad for placidity than tangible creatures of that ancient city. But this is not fair, they are placid, and I have been too long in this house alone. If autumn is a time of change, then winter is a time not to change. Or to change. My cats know the truth. Winter is for change, because no change is impossible. It is for lovers, and those left alone. Winter is for growth and death only. Be still.

CERTIFIED ALIVE

Four pound boots and two pound wool sweaters; everything is
heavy in winter. The physician's assistant deducts three pounds
off the scale for my quilted cargo pants & thick purple socks:
sweet, grandmotherly, even with a needle. Each spring I emerge
thicker with bear weight. My hair grows, my waist, my growl a
truer lament. Too many winters, too much weight. This is my
physical, I should be allowed to weep openly. It is a dirty busi-
ness, this winter, seeping shitty grainy slush by the back door.
Thermal inserts overtake sneakers—turn them into quaint coast-
ers for the work of burial, exhumation. This is the place where I
pee in a cup: the waste of whiskey and winter. It is taken, tested,
deemed healthy piss for the moment. I ask if they will carry it out-
side, proclaim my status in a yellow gush, *Certified Alive,* across the
pristine white snow. They will not, nor with my blood. It will take
till spring to spell the names of my discontent. And then melt.
Half pound hats, quarter pound gloves; it is a testament that we
climb out from under winter at all. Outside, the walk is buried
beneath a fresh ten inches of snow. The storms closed in again last
night, now later today, at some point, I must assemble my full win-
ter weight to shovel a way for the postman to deliver the last of my
test results. If I am too late, only his shadow will appear.

Weak Punch

The punches of March melt away as softly as they land. No featherweight nor boxer of any class; the lingering days practice yoga in limber rays, spry weekend joggers emerging on weakened ankles. They stretch themselves on street corners. March angry old man flails at warmer air evoking temper for maturity, for lots of things, too late to learn that fear for respect for love for lots of intangibles are not those intangibles, only fear, only more fear. March strength is gone; those baby punches almost kisses now, pitiful. Adoring light strobes gauzy yet you resist. Leave it, unlock your steps, it is okay to roll on mashed grass!

The Poet Washes Dishes

It took several hours. There were spaces in the cookware of which no one was aware, save the poet. The soft downturn of the ladle handle soared and fell like the epic point guard's final jump shot as the seconds die away... Water turned from periods to semi-colons and, finally, ellipses. If the sponge was wrung-out in the perfect combination of soap and water—the poet erupted into mirthful glee. Otherwise, tears. The poet shooed his wife away from the dirty dishes like an anthropologist hoarding the dirty femur of Java Man, stared out the window at the muddy March snow. He did not love the dishes; merely cherished them as a measure of time's elapse, a graceful collapse. Another chop gone by. The final swallow, the final tine, an expulsion of methane. As the last dish hit the rack the poet pondered the finality of one more meal; this all before dessert and coffee were even served. As always, it took a lifetime.

KINGDOM OF WORMS

GARBAGE OF THE GLITTERING SUN

Gentrified dog turds are the stucco of spring. I am wealthy beyond your ken: muddy vistas are my orchards squeezing liters of salt wine per loose clump. In my hut of earth and debris there is no need for napkins—we eat broken glass from leftover Genesee bottles, spit amber slivers into a cowering new orb of gas. Garbage of the glittering sun. Poke a hole in my Hefty windows and yank back a sandwich ass off the pissed-on spring curb. The due date is January, it is ripe and delicious! Lay your babies down in a field of used diapers, powder their crotches with milk duds and condoms. It is too late anyway. My feast is organic, partially digested. Allow me to gather you a bouquet of fudgicle sticks, cigarette filters, cracked prescription bottles, mildewed corn chips—I am a romantic and in love with the season. This is the story of March: if we fall in love it will be forever or until I find something better down the street. As if winter never existed, the world one glorious landfill! I promise you the best gravel you have ever tasted, my sweets. We will christen it Terra Firma.

KINGDOM OF WORMS

And beetles and grubs. And everything. The city left piles of autumn leaves; one thousand pounds of snow turning them into gelatinous muck ghettos on every curb. I wonder what crawls over what in there, this March, fat juiciest nutrients going where? Queen and King. Worker worm, sexy millipede. In this battle for existence servant ants drizzle water over soldier ants while concubines dream of being soldier ants and soldier ants dream of their next drizzle... Oily and meager. Everything comes before death. It is sunny and the world is dozing in filth: wear your boots and kick the shit out of a dying kingdom today. It is joy to be god-like just for fun. Lick a wasp stinger and listen to its secrets. Boil the hive for soup. Now you are ready to run for mayor of your own sweet dung heap. It is easy, if elected we promise to kick the shit out of every other dying kingdom until there is nothing left but this one of worms, scum of the earth, one deity and four baited hooks. We will hold a feast in his honor, don't you know? You are the main dish.

Instructions for a Rainy Day

Try this: Go outside in a rainstorm (legal disclaimer: Not a lightning storm). Easy, but not enough. Lie down in the largest open space that you can find. If you are lucky, there will be grass. If you are unlucky, you may be run over by a car or truck (legal disclaimer: Do not be). Despite the advice of natural selection and your mother—you are now flat on your back in a clearing in a rainstorm. How do you feel (that is a manipulative question, unfair, please disregard with my apologies)? Open your mouth. Open it wide. Imagine how many drops of water there are falling all around you. Try numbers. If you are a visual person imagine the size, shape, etc. of what they would fill. Name them all. Try to develop some sort of personal connection with each and every one (emotional disclaimer: Do not try to love them, they will only disappoint you). Now ask yourself, with these raindrops all around—why do so few enter my mouth?

FEAST OF THE WOUNDED BIRD
(from Marc Chagall's *The Wounded Bird*)

Early spring is late winter dying like a bird with an arrow through
its breast. Prancing days of sun pursue the bird; sprays of color
clump around our feet. This bird has been dying for seventy-five
years now—would gladly trade the harsh king of Corinth his
boulder, cruel Chagall. Splay your limbs, imagine unmixed hues
united. The beak of salvation, yellow snips, umber shadow,
motion in the sweep of tiny wisps, tiny wisps.

Formula for Frustration

Fewer gaps of light exist between people in the spring. Half a silhouette. More light, fewer spaces; the sun is selling but who isn't? One zinc penny dead in the morning is a poor symbol for the plight of humanity: the elements never breathed, though they may have been hated more than loved. More tellingly, ignored. I wheel out the courtyard table, oversized umbrella—yes, of course — chairs, never once asking them to do so themselves, a formula for frustration. I will sit in these for three seasons never mistaking them for the asshole who nicknamed me pork chop in little league. They will remain chairs, while he, most likely, makes more money than me, still the asshole. It is so easy losing grip of your emotions in spring, it's true. I am no Harry Crosby, but I appreciate good sunlight where I find it. Better half a silhouette than a whole.

AMERICAN PROSE POET

I love prose poetry but don't speak French. I don't speak anything
really. Mispronounce the great minds. That's an order. Say
Goethe like *Go The*. Say Ponge like *Sponge* with a *P*. Make Jacob an
Amish farmer. Go ahead, they're dead. Only the academics can
cut you now, and we all know about them—they eat canapes and
call it art. I stand under them; out of the cold April rain always
better. If you will pay my way I could become French in six
months: Swap Wonder for *pain*; shit for *merd*; Arch of Triumph
for *Arc de Triomphe*—*Voila!* I am a great lover encompassing pigeons
and wizened old women in one swath; you cannot resist my sub-
tle wit, yes? Take my hand, walk by the Erie Canal; it is cold again
and this month is full of war. So Goethe wasn't any more French
than your canape is Braque, professor. It all makes sense when the
bar lights shudder on. Now I am stuttering, stateside again,
moaning the brokedown blues....

TWENTY-SIX DAYS OF SUN

Twenty-six days of sun in six months. I don't know if he is
drunk or mentally unstable, but the man with the cat at the ani-
mal hospital is insane. My cat is dying today. His cat is dying
ahead of mine. He talks to his, while my cat and I stare out the
window trying not to listen. The thing itself is embarrassing. If
the sun comes out tomorrow, Whitman and I will take a walk. I
will point out babies, big brothers, immunize him to the cycle he
has unwittingly joined. The lines are so clean, the accoutrements
of veterinary medicine so sparse. A glass jar filled with cotton balls,
brown jar labeled "Alcohol," two more jars, swabs, swan-neck
faucet. In the background the receptionist maintains upbeat chatter
about a client cat's third eye looking so much better. Healed up.
No more third eye problems. I think: *Was I born here? Has my cat taken
me here to die instead?* If that is the case so be it: five months without
sun is too much to take. My son will take me to the woods and
leave me to die. It is the cycle we have unwittingly joined. If the
clouds clear away tomorrow, we will all go there together.

A Girl

A girl was a bicycle and she didn't like her paint. She liked her wheels but hated her reflectors. Her rims were slightly bent. This caused her great suffering. She stood on the curb of an endless bicycle parade, not a race, and each one glided past truer, smoother, and bolted tighter than she. Lamenting her poor drooping chain she beckoned a friend, *Be a baseball card. Ride in my spokes. Chatter as we go and surely they will not hear the squeaking of my joints.* But the friend turned into a kite and flew away. *You will be my streamers!* A man with a package and coattails just long enough to latch onto came close enough: *Be my streamers,* she demanded. *You will flutter in colors of the rainbow as I roll by and one day perhaps they will forgive the dullness of my hue.* But the man jumped into the package, sealed and mailed himself back home. *Mother,* she wept tilting onto her kick-stand, *Father,* she moaned crashing to the grass, *how could you saddle me with such a tattered seat, poor steering and undependable brakes? Surely you will become the orange flags trailing over my head pulling their eyes upward and away from the horrible flatness of my tires, this endless slow leak.* But her parents were a worm and a bird: one ate the other and gracefully alighted on a nearby tree branch, neatly preening. The girl rocked and put herself right, sadly rolling off down the street. All through the neighborhood one could hear the squeaking of her wheels, but grease would take years to find its way.

A Man Learns to Fly

In his younger years his father had toted him out to the bird feeder. It was brown, bent, speckled with white droppings—angled against all seasons. No mix was sufficient to keep the lesser birds away: Old bruise-colored grackles arrived on the scene. Meager starlings. Rusty female cardinals. At each new mix, elated, they waited, but the loveliest of feathered winds never blew their way. And so the father taught him to love the ugly ones. Named them after earls and dukes, invested them with flight patterns to shame the baldest of eagles.

In the boy's front yard, truly, the meek had inherited the earth.

Such is the ornithology of family.

A boy flew away one morning to return a man to find his father turned to ash beside a bag of grainy seeds. And this note: *Help me to fly.*

My Cat Recites A Poem

It is warm today, warm enough for the black cat to find a new
perch. He sits on the ledge, nose pressed to rusty window screen.
His tail curls into a smile surveying saucy birds and squirrels that
chittertaunt never once thinking to join in, satisfied to observe
through this thin crosshatch of weathered irony. He vomits there,
watches it. How like the poet he is.

KINGDOM OF THE SILVER HAIRBRUSH

1)

At the point of mortality freezing and burning are exactly the same. So arrived Doubting Thomas at the Doorstep of Believe. The oval shimmer. Vainglorious ambulation. The morning before the last glance at every relationship you've known will appear like this: respond in kind when the man on the bicycle rings his bell at you. This is the signal you've been waiting for. It rings between the gyrating molecules of your nervous tapping fingers. A belief that led Thomas to nightly brush his wife's sumptuous black hair one thousand times while a talisman circled overhead. Cried overhead. One revolution per stroke.

2)

The bat cracked at the top of the third; echoes shook Thomas across the outfield as he brushed his mother's hair with an heirloom silver brush. The brush was magical. The silver brush whispered of nobler births than this: cold peas in the freezer, a pan of urine under the mattress. *So arrived Doubting Thomas at the Doorstep of Believe.* In the meadow they played with dandelions chanting, "Mama had a baby and its head popped off" with the incantatory power of priests and priestesses.

3)

They were married in spring. Thomas was born six months later. Mourners doubted he was truly the son, the legitimate heir to the Kingdom of the Silver Hairbrush.

All was silent as the crown was settled on his head.

TEMPLE OF JUNE BUGS

◆ ◆ ◆

Waiting On A Friend

It is June, the wind tastes like butter, the road trip at an end.
Thank you, Cricket, for the free coffee in Ohio—I almost made
it, a hard life teaches true kindness. The Hyatt looks like home
from here, but that's merely an illusion of June too: interstates
writhing with the fear and guilt related to family and friends.
Because you ask I will tell you of the myth of linear time.
Huddled in the back seat each truck rumbles clots loose to the
heart: if I had been dreaming, nightmare, because I was awake,
reality. I held the crystal in my hand, was forced to believe things
I would rather not. Her name was Cricket. All friendship is dif-
ferent in summer. As for me, nothing would cure me—I had
taken it too far. Vertigo occurs on a daily basis, a hangover of too
many journeys into less-than-sanctioned time zones. The world
died. I explode into laughter each time I walk down the street.

The Wonderment We Bypassed

I built a city out of a strand of your hair but the bombs came and stripped all but the memory of your shampoo, the cigarette smoke of desert cafes; I won't believe you exist until I stride along your spine made of seashells. These decaying fossil bones of your past loves, a steaming broth of celery, mint and milk: meet me in billowy chambers devoted to meager forgetful angels. Angel necks, my own bare hands. Bones snapping like glass. My mouth will revive the city you never dreamed your head might create.

A Letter To My Love

This is generous of me, he said. Far beyond what most men would undertake. I am killing myself slowly weekend by weekend for you, he explained. There is a dialogue going on between us that you are not a part of. You will not allow yourself to see certain things, he said, so I am killing myself a little at a time to show you those things. Behold, this is what a future dead man looks like. See I am dead. See my pallor. How waxen. It is like a dandelion no one cares about. This is my metaphor, so pay close attention: I have been a dandelion no one cares about spraying myself with toxins to make me die until you came along with pig-tails bouncing and picked me and set me in a spaghetti sauce jar on your windowsill that light shines through and sometimes you touch me to your neck to test for butter compatibility and ticklishness but giggling you see this proves it: I ramble on so because I am a young man and always dying. There are signs. You will see it first in my lack of sympathy for myself and others. Dying men are always cruel. Oh how cruel they can be. And then I will turn inward and grasp for any lingering tangibles and then, finally, give up the ghost. When I am dead you will read back through this and someday you will understand that I loved you so much as to kill myself so slowly so that you would understand what I meant when I said that there are communications taking place between us that you will not allow yourself to understand. Do you now? Oh, my love my love. My sweet love is like a broomstick wrapped around your hair, gently sweeping.

Temple of June Bugs

I propose a marriage of youth and adulthood at the Temple of
June Bugs; our unborn children will bear flowers and rings.
Memory serves best the brooders and romantics, but to create
anew the romantic, the romantic. I fell in love with summer while
dancing together in a dusty field. Music sounds better in sum-
mer: each lyric, each note pricking the nape, revealing the ripe
chub dangling off ten-pound test line as constant companion. We
are all Tom Sawyer. Blue bicycle, weedy hills, one time to play
grass like a kazoo, one to remember those long days playing. My
summer lodge is a rock in the mouth of the Saint Lawrence
Seaway. Hold my hand beneath the table, this honeymoon, no
one will see us fall on our backs as meteors shower overhead....

Checking On Whitman

His bedroom is warm, black: the last gasp of air before diving
down through a deep summer lake to listen to the heart beat. His
own, the last he will ever need. I call it mine, but it is no more
mine than the mint mist at the base of a great falls belongs to
the river that brought it. He was gone with a sigh, a moan,
enough for a lifetime....

Puberty (Our Arms & Legs Emerge)

On the last day of school Dougie told Francie he would send
tooth chippings, shed body parts from summer camp. He grew
busy corralling ants on the dock into spilled Bain de Soleil;
unaware of Buddhist considerations he lost his first girlfriend to
a stout catcher named Tiny. In summer, somewhat embarrassed,
our arms and legs emerge. The tradeoff, each season we become
more and less ourselves, remembering that forgotten. And for
good reason! In retrospect, reassuring the ant its struggle is
greater than its goal seems cruel. It was only a summer romance:
caresses, promises, pop music, the works, parting as summer too
licked its salty gash to a close. Nothing is beyond hope, even
more so in the sunlight. On the last day of summer Tiny told
Francie they were through. All good things lead to all good
things, she nodded, this thing too must end in sorrow and mem-
ory, one season in many seasons, a change better left to wait.

BEACH HEAD

I will fill my mouth with salt and let it trickle out until a new beachhead forms embracing the ocean, reading the same books as me. My time is my own. It is finite but longer than my eyes can follow: my breadbasket Atlantic, oily and gruff, sauté yourself in garlic, de-vein your denizens and pack my belly till slumber, it will take only seconds to swim you as idea. I hereby propose this: chop down every tree in the Amazon. We will build a plank bridge across the Atlantic gasping for breath as we cross it off our To Do list—larger challenges remain on the horizon. The light beer at lunch will save me enough calories at dinner to devour a whole school of baby manatees without guilt. A flock or a murder? Dipped in butter, eighty-two degrees and sunny. Let's get high on the flesh of amphibians.

The Dog Goes Bow-wow

The sound was not the normal sound: pulverized gold dust powdering country pathways, a wily purple scrawl inscribing a letter, bond, resolution, a treatise; the sound of things torn open and left behind. The sound was the sound of something incongruous but it wasn't the tearing that was odd. The tearing was tearing. Paper tearing: plastic/paper torn jaggedly, slantwise, honest. All the usual sounds and sensations were there and easily categorized. Once the light-switch makes its accepted "click" and the cat goes "meow" and bare feet pull free of hardwood in the usual "slap-pat" it's assumed that the nature of a whisper will not be that of a turbine and tangerines will never degrade into sonata. And now you: you at your desk at work, at your desk at work, you are not yet ready for lunch but you are hungry for a snack near ten-thirty, and you: you open your metal drawer expecting the usual "squeak" when a muted Paganini concerto emerges. And your question when the clock starts belching and the nimbus clouds recite scripture. When milk demands coffee, two sugars: do you shore up your nerve and ask if you are the exception when a paper clip falls and explodes into bowling balls: is it you or is it them? And if so how many of each. And when you are lying in a bed that becomes a jewelry box full of white cotton—parallel toes and heads gnashing live red and green electrical wires—and a torn condom wrapper dropped at the bedside floor screams in terror: is it time then to declare open legs to be the greatest prophets? To divine the truth of circumstance through invisible veins on closed eyelids? And will we do this now together.

Or shall we just go on pretending.

Peter Means Rock

Afloat on an ocean of accolades my largest medal will always spell out my geography. This is the city my friends remember to leave: whiskey and winter, twenty-six days of sun. We are all the same, affirmation only a phone-call away. When the polar caps melt the Front Range will be beachfront; miles of burning wilderness extinguished. California is Atlantis deep with veins of post-Apocalyptic gold: Silicone. I do what I can. They do not see me in this garden, my cinnamon arm a transport for peripatetic forms, pulling the weeds, trimming the shrubs, oblivious to Latinate Gary Snyder would savor, deliver. Peter means Rock. My thumb is brown, green, dozens have used it to measure vast distances, hitchhike to sprout in new earthen plots. Place to nose and flick.

CHROMO BOY

Chromo Boy awakes one rainy summer morning to find the wet pants still dirty on the line, a bag of garbage stinking up the kitchen floor. Paw prints in the sugar bowl. The writers of his generation have become the writers of his generation; no new star is born in the mailbox today. Each Sunday Chromo Boy cuts the eyes out of the youngest full-color literary prodigy and parades down to the café for free muffins and margarine. He is redeemed, fed, humiliated all for the price of one New York Times: too expensive, the system sucks. He drives a wedge into the mouth of the machine—open wide—so that others may have this news for free. Built-in walls filled with vacant eyes, the mounted heads of ivy-league copywriters. Ads for Chromo he is learning to forget. No new stars were born today, his headline, and the planets we dream to visit are in a distant galaxy, far far away....

What Will You Do For Me?

If I slice the space around me. If I do this for you. If I carve into matter severing it from the perceptions of, say, Enrique, Mardou, Lionel, and, Mary and serve it back up to you on a bed of foam and spring: will we believe it possible to be so together? Because this is the thing you must know and never reveal. The apple core. A face on the milk. The slow disgrace of leaves wilting into nutrient. I was eight years old when the old man on the park bench opened wide and swallowed me whole. A feeding frenzy. Today I notice the blood beneath the bones more than the bones beneath the flesh and the flesh not at all. Blood is always swelling, pulsing for release. The apple core, the milk, a candy bar for dessert: the ultimate state of mud. Walking thru parking lots of long closed gas stations and empty tailor shops I am humbled by the hollow quiver: on the left the all-night deli is slicing ham; layering it thick for smoking school boys and plumping girls. On the right I move proud and hungry, cloaking myself in this empty space, paring it down to the finish line. And still, if I take you withering to see it. If I tear this space around us and offer up these tender victuals. If I do this for you tell me.

The Great Undertoad of Cape Cod

I've had it pointed out countless times but still can't identify poison ivy, or won't. Grains of sand freckled with dry black seaweed. Illusory cerulean sky with single billowing pillar of cloud, more smoke than air: childish fears are amusing. My friend, Andy, grew up afraid of the great horny toad lurking to pull him under the ocean waves. Were there millions, thousands, or just one waiting for him? The one that counts, this fear of our names forgotten. European girls work the cash registers, the deli counters, nameless for the first time in their lives, trying out their American English slang—a crash course in the commerce of flip-flops and indolence. Only the itch is real. A tongue will never reach as far as the insinuation of a tongue, the pull of the ocean never as great as that of the word alone.

Dog Days

I admit I have used the term without knowing its origin. But the Egyptians liked cats, right? Of course, there are other ancients, but the Egyptians were by far the most summery. Now that Sumeria is American I can ignore Egyptians past and present— concentrate on smaller issues like tan lines, golf shirts, honeymoons and vacations. My suv could kill twenty languorous winter cats beneath its wheels on one tank of gas, unleaded, en route to Nantucket. And yet. The dog days of summer are good for nothing if not for this: Sirius, lead star of Canis Major, ascendant into heaven and seated at the right hand of the Father, unleashed and drooling. The Greeks were great classifiers, but the Egyptians knew how to throw a party! Rich soil, high water, the Nile on the rise: the Egyptians danced and screwed while Northerners scanned the Dog Star for the new name of civilization.

IN THE BARN

But Not Today

I walk with Whitman over a bed of sad potato chips giggling at the music of mutinous early autumn. One day the yellow buses will carry us away....

The Thing Behind the Other Thing

One night before bed a man decided to make brown sugar toast. He prepared the bread with butter, sprinkled it with brown sugar and inserted it into the toaster on the counter beside a radio. The cat slept on top of a heating vent just outside the kitchen entry-way. Every so often its whiskers twitched. The man ignored the cat. He watched the rain fall outside. He turned on the radio and listened to a local psychotherapist identifying the symptoms of a seasonal diagnosis. The man removed the sugar toast; he crunched it while the psychotherapist enunciated the word, *Malaise.*

♦

A man and his cat were eating supper at the same time. They were both in the kitchen. The man was eating soup, the cat was crunching dry food provided by the man. At intervals, the cat would drink water from a bowl. Often during dinner the man would play a call-in program through the radio across the kitchen on the counter beside the toaster oven. This night he did not listen although he nodded sometimes as if he were listening. There was agreement in the air. The man ate his soup. The cat crunched his food.

♦♦

A man walked on a treadmill in his living room in front of a television program. The cat regarded the man. The man had only recently started walking this way. The man purchased a pair of athletic shorts, a pair of white socks and some blue running sneakers. An old undershirt was just fine. The man walked each day for forty-five minutes. He had begun walking for only fifteen minutes but sticking strictly to a regimen he had built up to forty-five minutes. In the future, he thought, he may walk for even longer.

◆◆◆

A man and his cat looked out the window. The rain had come to each window of the house. The cat's thoughts were inaccessible to the man. *It is nothing if not treachery*, said the man aloud. The man's words were inaccessible to the cat. *But seasonal depression is our birthright*, said the man, *floral shops weary of dead roses.* Then the man stopped saying things and, for a period, only thought.

The cat licked one paw balanced on the tripod of three other paws. The licked paw curled inward.

Huey

Huey ran with scissors in his mouth. He was not chosen for
dodge ball. There was paste on his breath, urine on his sneaker,
dirt inside his ears—he grew potatoes in there. He was that boy.
He always came out wrong. On the Monday morning in question
he held his head but left his stomach open. They did not kick his
stomach. A kick in the ass is funny. Funnier yet: a kick in the
balls. Huey was a green boy. They called him a yellow boy. He lay
on the ground. His books were the audience. Huey was an orange
boy. He ran with scissors in his mouth and paste in his mouth
and raspberry scented non-toxic markers in his mouth. Huey
smelled like dried sweat. He was orchid, purplish. Monday morn-
ing they kicked him through the final spectrum. They were going
for the laugh. Huey was a red boy curled on the sidewalk. A dead
brown leaf in the October sun.

In the Barn

Of course I could mention sunlight filtering through the space between boards. The sunlight could fall on hay—fresh hay, the whole organic mess. It could beam off the tine of a pitchfork. But I want my pitchfork rusty. A symbol of toil, honesty, age, remorse. The sun is beaming. It illuminates a knothole in a floorboard containing a tenpenny nail that has never been struck. The nail is protected by the knothole. Pristine. Never been soiled. Never been used. Neglected. Forgotten. Ineffectual. The nail is a laughing angel in the sunlight; sunlight that filters in through an oblong knothole in the wall pinpointing the knothole on the floor that contains the manger of the baby Jesus. The baby Jesus holds out a tenpenny nail; a matter of prophecy. Go forth. He will build mangers out of wood until he is crucified at thirty-three: decent carpenter, outstanding martyr. Without motion sunlight cannot dapple. Unfortunate, as who can resist a moment of dappling sunshine? In the autumn of our lives? Bountiful as they may be. Amen. Motes of dust may filter through the sunlight. Before it a tiny fist emerges out of a knothole on the floor—it makes the sign of the cross at you before you ever sneeze. Lord almighty. He is good. A neglected milk bucket, a horseshoe, a hayloft, a grain shoot, a tomcat, a leaky roof, mouse skeleton, a pick ax, a hoe; the whole bawling shithouse sprawl of the productivity of the people of the earth.

God bless it all, god damn it.

Moonlight falls.

Nature Walk

The cobweb stretched between two rocks creating a nine-inch death net. The lake did what lakes do: sit there and look nice until they freeze into brumous tombs. It was not yet frozen. Too warm still with fall grasping the retreating leg of summer while winter put its first boot to the weak chin of autumn. He was no stupid cricket or fly or whatever spiders eat. Who cared? He hooked his toe under the web, between the rocks, and brought it up slowly, venomously, thinking perhaps he was moving as slowly as the spider had when it spun the thing out its ass. Or whatever they do. He unzipped his pants and pissed on a pine cone as a heron took flight in a stand of cattails....

It was all too much to take.

Beyond The Dream

The first homeless man on the moon was not allowed into the planning sessions that brought him to the position. He was simply the first homeless man on the moon. That was thought to be enough. He did not like the packets of dried fruits. The salted nuts made him constipated. This was also ancillary to the proceedings. The first homeless man on the moon was part of a broad-based constituency of fearless pioneers who would colonize the moon. As with all tourists, the constituency was most interested in that which was most familiar. Potholes were constructed. Locks were placed on all doors, then broken into, then, following neighborhood meetings lamenting the decay of moon society, repaired. Alarms were installed. The mayor of the moon became embroiled in scandal. His campaign was hindered, but his image was restored. The first homeless man on the moon was not able to vote in mayoral elections. The mayor was elected, that was enough. Elevators rose to the top of tall buildings. A beauty queen was installed. As time passed, more and more homeless people landed on the moon. What made the first one so special? The moon was a wonderful place, after all, but not nearly so lovely as Mars.

Max

Swells within the ballroom of the belly too soon to drop down pink and white through bloody shadows of October reacquainting us with one true statement. The only one. I pray he will have more brains than originality—that relentless picture of Einstein's mealy tongue elongated beneath tufted gray mustache. The Creator of the A-bomb was a pacifist: he will pay for that with slivers of his dignity. Brains are commonly worshipped; originality only if money never changes hands. And only after death. Max will scream into October through his entire life. He must learn to scream quietly though, intelligently. Proprietary not incendiary—that's the way. Perhaps one day he can be forgotten altogether.

GATHERING

Our bodies have been sliced to decaying confetti. It is so common as to be universal. Flaps of skin follow us from apartment to apartment; a DNA breadcrumb trail. Most scars on our bodies are as mysterious as the trials that brought us here. A bolt of lightning down the thumb. A pit in the cheek. As teenagers my best friend opened my forearm with a hunting knife until we saw white. I did the same to him. Fiery drops of melting plastic. A stick in the forehead. We disfigured each other like Masai warriors; dragging boars from the mundanity of cul-de-sac wilderness. I have no stories to tell. My body celebrates my existence by chopping itself and leaving pieces for you to read. Tea leaves. Thrown bones. My nose falls off when it rains.

DROPPING

Theo was well past frustration, into fascination. The option was insanity. He hadn't been able to hold an object, any object, in his hands for over a year now. Imagine! An entire year without grasping, clutching or squeezing anything. Opposable thumbs be damned! Theo was astounded. The doctors scratched their chins, muttered terms, wondered aloud about diagnoses that were soon dismissed. They pricked each finger on each hand and, like anyone, Theo yelled out. They handed him tongue depressors that fell. They sent him to psychiatrists who asked him about shapes and impressions, any lingering malaise. Nothing. Theo was given prescriptions—they stuffed them into his jacket pockets but the orders were never filled. No pills, Theo said, they won't help. It went on and on like this for months until Jill, Theo's wife, left him. Thirteen months of affliction, she said, she couldn't take it; was leaving him for a mechanic named Hank who could dress and feed himself. Hank fixed Volvos. Nice reliable cars. So what to do? Theo looked himself in the mirror and asked this question aloud daily. It hung fixed in the air.

DIAGNOSIS

A little spackle, a fresh coat of paint—new meat on them bones.
We select one poignant age and return to it each year. Your cards
are empty now, lanky puppy, but your mind remains fixed on the
treat. The author of this poem was born September 11, 1970 in a
small town named America. That century seems like a century
away. Did Jack the Ripper give birth to it? Perhaps—my memory
doesn't care. This isn't about ego. The title of this story is *I Am
Perpetually Fourscore and Three Years Older Than the 21st Century But
Always Sixteen in my Mind.* The year I learned to drive. To get the
fuck away from you. If you light candles on cakes or anywhere
this year you will remain trapped in the terrible twos: pissing
yourself, crying, lashing out for naught worth shit in your diaper.
Blow out those candles—this is no trick. Be quiet, go to sleep. It
will all look different in the gloaming.

REJOICE

Postcards, gas bills, love letters tinged with pheromones. I don't know whether it is an act of trust or a test of loyalty but people keep giving me things to mail. This is too much though. Marked undeliverable. Instead I will sit here dreaming of packages that open into a future they will never reveal. Only ritual, only more ritual: cats and dogs poised to hear bell chimes through a shifting maze of seasons. This nip in the air. Temple of June Bugs, Kingdom of Worms; the time of our awaited birth is awash in new currents, baptized in rivers of whiskey and winter. Strange flowers planted to pick or plow under. As you will.

About the Author

Peter Conners is author of four collections of poetry and prose including *Emily Ate the Wind* (Marick Press, 2008). He is founding co-editor of *Double Room: A Journal of Prose Poetry & Flash Fiction,* which has been published online by Web del Sol since 2001. He also edited *PP/FF: An Anthology* which was published by Starcherone Books in 2006.

Peter lives in Rochester, New York with his wife, Karen, a clinical psychologist, and three children, Whitman, Max, and Kane. He works as an editor and oversees marketing for BOA Editions.

His web site is: www.peterconners.com.

White Pine Press and the author
thank the following individuals
for their generous support
in the publication of this collection:

June Baker
Dan Cawley & Paula Baker
Stephen & Violanda Burns
P. David & Eleanor Caccamise
Gwen & Gary Conners
Gregory & Jan Conners
Mark & Karen Conners
William DeLamarter
Scott & Carol Falso
Greenwood Books/ Franlee Frank
Jason Garrison
Kelsie Harder
Tim & Shannon Hay
Stanley & Pat Kazmerski
Todd Weiner & Linda Kilanoski
Andy & Margret McDermott
Stephen & Michelle Michel
Chris & Pamela Pollack
Karl & Julia Postler
Stephen & Heather Ralph
Stephen Kennedy Robinson
Nan & Dan Westervelt
The Vogt Family
Kasey, Peter & Taryn Ward
Craig & Rebecca Westervelt